MY CHRISTMAS BOOK

Myrrh and Aloes and Cassia

Out of the Ivory Palaces

Ring out, ye Ancient Steeples;
Bid all earth's Scattered Peoples
Rejoice with one accord!
For on this Wondrous Christmas morn,
A Little Child to us is born
A Savior, Christ the Lord!

MY CHRISTMAS BOOK

A Handful of Myrrh, Aloes and Cassia

F. W. BOREHAM

John Broadbanks Publishing
Eureka, CA 2015

John Broadbanks Publishing
Eureka, CA
2015

10 9 8 7 6 5 4 3
Printed in the United States of America

ISBN: 978-0-9832875-9-9
eISBN: 978-0-9832875-8-2

Cover Design: Laura Zugzda
Layout: Marcia Breece
eBook: Marcia Breece

PUBLISHED BY

JOHN BROADBANKS PUBLISHING

F. W. BOREHAM

Second Thoughts–Introduction by Ravi Zacharias (2007)

A Packet of Surprises: The Best Essays and Sermons of F. W. Boreham (2008)

Angels, Palms and Fragrant Flowers: F. W. Boreham on C. H. Spurgeon (2009)

Lover of Life: F. W. Boreham's Tribute to His Mentor (Revised and Expanded) (2009)

All the Blessings of Life: The Best Stories of F. W. Boreham (Revised) (2010)

Loose Leaves: A Travel Journal (2010)

Loose Leaves eBook (2010)

All the Blessings of Life eBook (2010)

In Pastures Green: A Ramble through the Twenty-third Psalm (2011)

The Chalice of Life: Reflections on the Significant Stages in Life (Second Edition) (2012)

From England to Mosgiel (2012)

Lover of Life eBook (2013)

The Coming of Snowy (2015)

GEOFF POUND

Making Life Decisions: Journey in Discernment (2009)

Talk About Thanksgiving: Stories of Gratitude (2010)

How F. W. Boreham Won the War of Words (2014)

JEFF CRANSTON

Happily Ever After: Studies in the Beatitudes (2010)

Contents

BY WAY OF INTRODUCTION

A Child Is Born! That Is Forever and Forever
The Message of Christmas.

A Child is born! In the early days of the nineteenth century, men were following with bated breath the march of Napoleon and waiting with feverish impatience for the latest news of the wars. And all the while, in their own homes, babies were being born. Just think of some of those babies. Why, in one year, lying midway between Trafalgar and Waterloo, there stole into the world a host of heroes! During that year, 1809, Mr. Gladstone was born at Liverpool; Alfred Tennyson drew his first breath at the Somersby rectory; and Oliver Wendell Holmes made his initial appearance in Massachusetts. On the very self-same day of that self-same year, Charles Darwin made his debut at Shrewsbury and Abraham Lincoln in Old Kentucky. Music was enriched by the advent of Frederick Chopin at Warsaw and Felix Mendelssohn at Hamburg.

But nobody thought of babies. Everybody was thinking of battles. Yet, viewing that age in the truer perspective which the years enable us to command, we may well ask ourselves which of the battles of 1809 mattered more than the babies of 1809. When a wrong wants righting, or a work wants doing, or a truth wants preaching, or a continent wants opening, God sends a baby into the world to do it. This is why, long, long ago, a Babe was born at Bethlehem.

—**F. W. BOREHAM**
Kew
Victoria
Australia

MYRRH

A Midsummer Christmas

The Old Doctor's Last Christmas

Three Pretty Maids

How Christmas Came to Roaring Camp

A MIDSUMMER CHRISTMAS

CHRISTMAS COMES BUT ONCE A YEAR. Indeed, there are those who doubt whether, on this side of the world, it comes as often as that. To folk who were reared in the older lands, and even to those who, through the medium of a wealthy literature, have imbibed the spirit of the traditional Yuletide, a midsummer Christmas must always seem a weird kind of hotch-potch.

Southey avers that, however long a man lives, the first twenty years of his life will always be the larger half of it. In a sense, this assertion is sound. 'The thoughts of youth are long, long thoughts.' The opening years of life fasten upon our hearts sentiments and impressions that will dominate all our days. There are vast numbers of Australians who, whenever they find old Father Christmas wiping the perspiration from his brow as he wanders among the roses and strawberries of an antipodean summertime, feel secretly sorry for him. He seems to be casting about for snowflakes and icicles and finding only ice creams.

Every Englishman settled in Australia cherishes in his heart a fond, though frantic, hope. He knows that it can never be realized: the stars in their courses are fighting against him; he is but crying for the moon. Yet, even though he is permitted to spend a hundred summers beneath these sunny skies, he will never quite relinquish that pleasing and passionate illusion. He will steal furtively to the window every Christmas morning and will throw up the blinds to see if at last, at last, his dream has all come true. How he would love to see the whole horizon a sheet of dazzling whiteness! He wants the snow; the graceful, fluttering snow; the deep and drifting snow; and, however long he lives, Christmas will never be Christmas to him without it.

I

It is Christmas Eve. In the brightly blossoming hibiscus that screens my open-air sanctum, a blackbird is singing a Christmas carol of his own. Surrounded by a riot of roses, hollyhocks, carnations, phlox and begonias, I sit here in shirtsleeves with my paper spread out before me.

Although I have spent nearly three score Christmases under the Southern Cross, I have never completely resigned myself to celebrating Christmas at midsummer and have never quite recovered from the shock that I sustained when that strange experience first befell me.

As we approached the first Christmas after our wedding—my second Christmas in New Zealand:

my wife's first—the thought of spending the festive season by our two homesick selves grew increasingly intolerable. But whom could we invite?

Our manse had been built for us on virgin soul that had never been so much as scratched since the world began. Seth Draper, a massive Irishman, had offered, in the goodness of his heart, to break it up for us and the crop of vegetables that he coaxed from that tiny strip of territory looked like something out of a fairytale.

Seth was a great man in every way. He was well over six feet in height and was broadband massive in proportion. He was a lonely man. For many years he had been the sole support of his aged mother and invalid sister. He was only a laborer; his earnings were not large; the sister involved him in doctors' bills and chemists' bills; and poor Seth felt that, with his hands so full, he must steel his heart against all thoughts of homemaking on his own account.

He took no part in the social life of the church or the town, and most people thought him morose, reserved and gloomy. He was most faithful, however, in his attendance at the weeknight prayer meeting. One evening, acting upon a sudden impulse, I asked him if he would lead us to the Throne of Grace. A moisture came to his eyes. Did I think him worthy of that? Nay, but he could not do it if he would. And then, after a pause, would I give him a week to think about it? It was a wonderful prayer that Seth offered the following week.

It seemed as though the very depths were broken up; and a brave, unselfish heart yielded its hidden treasure. Seth's great gift in this connection became notorious; and they were memorable prayer-meetings in which he could be induced to take part.

Seth's mother and sister passed away within a few weeks of each other. When I saw the door of his trim little cottage standing open of an evening, and learned that Seth was at home, I often sauntered across the fields for a chat. A skillful gardener, he liked to talk about his flowers. One summer evening, about the middle of December, I took the mistress of the manse with me on one of these informal calls. Pitying his loneliness, and seized by a sudden inspiration, she invited him to come across to the manse on Christmas Day and share our dinner with us. He seemed pleased and readily agreed to come. But when the day arrived he appeared more taciturn than usual. He took little part in the conversation, and we were half sorry that we had brought to our board so dismal a guest.

II

After dinner we lounged in deck chairs on the verandah, enjoying the sunshine and strawberries-and-cream. And then, when the mistress of the manse had withdrawn to attend to household matters, he found his tongue and startled me. Did I know Elsie Hammond! Of course I did! Elsie was one of the most devoted workers in the church. She had come to Mosgiel from an orphanage years before. She had lived a hard life in her younger days, and it had left its mark upon her. But she had been for years in service at the doctor's; they were very kind to her; and she had come to be regarded as an integral part of the establishment. Having no home of her own, she made a home of the church. Her whole heart was in it. Whenever something special needed to be done, we all turned instinctively to Elsie. Everybody loved her, and I believe that any of the girls in her class would have laid down their lives for her. Did I know Elsie? What a question! But why did he ask?

He told me. He was lonely. Since his mother and sister died, he had had nothing and no one to live for. And somehow, he thought that Elsie was lonely; and he knew that she was good. He had never spoken to her, beyond mere formal words of greeting. He had never had anything to do with women-folk; and he didn't know how to start now. And, anyhow, in a little place like Mosgiel, it might look silly, and people would talk; and he would not for worlds make her uncomfortable.

I asked him if he had any reason to suppose that his admiration for Elsie was reciprocated.

'No,' he said, sadly, 'none at all. One Sunday afternoon, a month or two ago, I was coming up the road, and, looking over my shoulder, I saw Elsie coming a hundred yards or so behind me. She had another of the teachers with her. I had a scarlet nasturtium in my coat; I took it out and dropped it purposely. I glanced back to see if she picked it up; but she only kicked it into the grass by the side of the path.'

The case certainly did not look promising; but, at his urgent request, I undertook to see Elsie and sound her on the subject.

III

For a day or two I felt very perturbed, and wondered how on earth I should approach the delicate theme. But my worry, like most worries, was quite superfluous. My task was made wonderfully simple. On the following Sunday—the last day of the old year—Elsie dropped in after church. It was a perfect summer evening, and, after laying her Bible, her handbag and her gloves on the dining room table, she and the mistress of the manse sauntered off into the garden to look at the roses. I was tired after a heavy day, and threw myself for a moment on the couch. Absentmindedly, I reached out my hand and picked up Elsie's Bible. As I opened it, there fluttered from among its pages a pressed nasturtium! I saw my chance.

The ladies returned; one went off to get the supper, and I was left alone with the other. I at once asked her to tell me about the nasturtium in her Bible. Her utter confusion told me all that I wished to know.

'Elsie,' I said, seeing that she was unlikely to speak, 'Seth Draper dropped that flower; you kicked it into the grass by the side of the road; and then went back afterwards and picked it up and pressed it!'

She was amazed at discovering that I possessed the first half of the secret. To set her at her ease, I had to tell her how the information came to me. I do not flatter myself that the attempt to put her at her ease was altogether a success. But, however that may be, Seth and Elsie were happily married a few months later. When I left Mosgiel they had quite a little family around them, and, to this day, whenever our New Zealand letters contain any reference to any of the Drapers, our minds rush back to that first Christmas dinner in our Mosgiel manse.

THE OLD DOCTOR'S LAST CHRISTMAS

IT WAS CHRISTMAS DAY—AND A SUNDAY. The glen lay deep in snow. Dr. Davidson, the old minister, had, Ian Maclaren tells us, preached in the church in the morning, had visited some sick and lonely folk in the afternoon, and now, at night, was entertaining his trusted elder, Drumsheugh, at the manse. All at once he became strangely introspective and retrospective.

'You and I, Drumsheugh,' he observed solemnly, 'will have to go a long journey soon and give an account of our lives at Drumtochty. Perhaps we have done our best as men can, and I think we have tried; but there are many things we might have done otherwise, and some we ought not to have done at all. It seems to me now that the less we say in that day of the past the better. We shall wish for mercy rather than justice, and'—here the doctor looked earnestly over his glasses at his elder— 'we would be none the worse, Drumsheugh, of a friend to say a good word for us both in the Great Court!'

It was the doctor's last conversation. He saw his guest to the door, watched him vanish in the snow; returned to the fireside; and, when his old servant entered the room next morning, the doctor was sitting

cold and silent in his chair. He had slipped away with
the Christmas music still ringing in his ears.

I

'We would be none the worse of a friend to say a good
word for us in the Great Court!' The Bible contains two
stories—one near its beginning and one near its end—
which should be laid side by side. The *first* is the story
of a man who feels that he is suffering more than his
share of the slings and arrows of outrageous fortune.
He thinks of God as above the clouds, above the stars,
above everything, God is very high and very holy, too
wise to err and too good to be unkind; yet Job cannot
shake from his mind the conviction that God has
misunderstood him. And, in his agony, he cries out for
an arbitrator who can intervene between his tortured
soul and the God who seems to be so angry with him.
Oh, for one a little less divine than God, yet a little less
human than himself, who could act as an adjudicator,
an umpire, a mediator between them!

But neither the heavens above nor the earth
beneath can produce one capable of ending the painful
controversy. '*There is no arbiter who can come between
us and lay his hand upon us both,*' Job could find no

friend to say a good word for him in the Great Court.

The *second* story—the story from the end of the Bible—is the story of an old minister whose lifework is finished. Writing in reminiscent vein to a young minister, who is just beginning, he earnestly refers to his own ordination. To what, he asks, was I ordained an apostle? He answers his own question. He was ordained to proclaim to men the twin facts that 'there is one God and one Mediator between God and men, the man Christ Jesus.' A Court! And a Friend in the Great Court!

II

In one respect these two thinkers, standing with the long, long file of centuries between them, agree precisely; in one respect they differ sharply. Both subscribe to the affirmation: There is one God! It is faith's irreducible minimum. The Saracens sweep across the world, overthrowing the Christian Churches. But they march to the battle cry, 'There is one God, and Mohammed is His Prophet.'

There is one God! Up to that point Christian and Muslim are at one. It is the link that unites all priesthoods and all altars. There is one God! It may be hard to believe; it is harder still to disbelieve. Men feel that to reject that simple yet stupendous affirmation is to shut themselves up in a purposeless universe, the puppets of Chance and the playthings of Fate.

The man whose spiritual pilgrimage has led him to an unwavering conviction that there is one God is not very far from the Kingdom of Heaven. If I had my ministry over again, I would talk more about God. Not about His works or His ways, His power or His bounty. But about His very self—His omnipresence, His omniscience, His omnipotence; His unutterable goodness, His ineffable holiness, His splendor, His glory, His love. For if I could make men very sure of God, they would soon cry out, like Job, for a mediator who could reconcile them to Him.

So far Job and Paul agree. But, later, they part company. There is one God but no Mediator, cries Job in despair. There is one God and one Mediator, cries Paul in delight. None! One! The difference between Job's 'none' and Paul's 'one' is a difference of millions. None means nothing; one means everything. None means failure; one means felicity. None means perdition; one means paradise. The difference between 'no Mediator' and 'one Mediator' is a difference that can never be worked out by arithmetic.

One God and one Mediator! It is the glory of our humanity that it needs both. Man needs a God, and is restless and ill at ease until he finds Him. Man is so made that he must eat—and breathe—and sleep—and worship. The instinct of adoration is in our blood, and we are fretful and fevered until we find One at whose feet we can lay the tribute of our devotion. We need a Mediator, too, and are at our best when we recognize and confess our need of Him.

We know how Dr. Davidson died. I said that his conversation with Drumsheugh was his last. I was mistaken. His last conversation was with Skye, his dog. When John, the servant, paid his usual visit to the study before he went to his bed, the doctor did not hear him enter the room. He was holding converse with Skye, who was seated on a chair, looking very wise and deeply interested.

'Ye're a bonnie beastie, Skye,' exclaimed the doctor, 'for a' thing He made is verra gude. Ye've been true and kind to your master, Skye, and ye 'ill miss him if he leaves ye. Some day ye 'ill die also, and they 'ill bury ye, and I doubt that 'ill be the end o' ye, Skye! Ye never heard o' God, Skye, or the Savior, for ye're just a puir doggie; but your master is minister of Drumtochty and—a sinner saved by grace!'

Those were his last words. In the morning the doctor was still sitting in his big chair, and Skye was fondly licking a hand that would never again caress him.

Skye, the noblest dog in the world, had no sense of sin and no sense of grace, no need of a God and no need of a Savior!

Dr. Davidson, Skye's master, is a sinner saved by

grace. And it is his sense of sin and his sense of grace, his need of a God and his need of a Savior, that remove him by whole infinities from the faithful brute on the chair. Herein lies a profound truth. A few generations back, our fathers used to sing a hymn that would fall strangely upon modern ears.

What comfort can a Savior bring
To those who never felt their woe?
A sinner is a sacred thing,
The Holy Ghost hath made him so.

When the soul feels after God and the heart cries out for a Savior, it is proof positive of the divinity that dwells within us.

III

One God—just one! And one Mediator—just one! But the beauty of it is that one is enough. One is often an abundance. It is only in the minor matters of human experience that we crave the privilege of picking and choosing; in the really vital things of life we are content with satisfaction. When the appetite is cloyed and sated, and food is a matter of indifference, we like to be invited to choose from an array of tempting foods; but when a man is ravenous he ceases to be fastidious. Set food before him and he is content. The hiker, walking for pleasure, likes to choose between several alluring trails; the pilgrim desires only the road that leads home. The globe-trotter lingers over the various shipping lists; the castaway longs but to sight a single sail. In the hour of our desperate need, felicity lies in simplicity.

No man, yearning after God as the deer pants after the water brooks, will resent the statement that there is but one God and but one Mediator. Such a seeker will not quote the words as though they expressed some element of stinginess in the pantheon of the universe, some miserly frugality in the eternal scheme of things. It will not suggest to him that the world contains a surplus of goods, but a deficiency of gods. He feels that he does not need a host of gods if he has the God of Hosts. Indeed, he is relieved by his very immunity from the necessity of choice. Multiplicity would mean perplexity. The benighted wayfarer dreads the place where the roads fork. The man who, weighted with his consciousness of spiritual need, hungrily desires salvation, is glad that there is but one God and but one Mediator.

For most of us the issue is clarified by the fact that there is but one Name given under heaven among men whereby we must be saved. While it would be an unspeakable calamity if there were no God and no Mediator, it is a source of adoring gratification that there is but one. The difference between no God and one God, between no Savior and one Savior, is a difference so stupendous that all the immensities and infinities seem to repose within it.

THREE PRETTY MAIDS

IT IS CHRISTMAS EVE; AND, FROM the room opposite, there float to me the rollicking strains of Christmas music. The young people, running the gamut of the old-time carols—*God Rest Ye Merry, Gentlemen, The First Noel, Good King Wenceslas,* and the rest—have reached the jingle about the three little ships—

> *Three little ships came sailing by,*
> *Sailing by, sailing by;*
> *Three little ships came sailing by,*
> *On Christmas Day in the morning.*
> *What do you think was in those ships,*
> *In those ships, in those ships?*
> *What do you think was in those ships,*
> *On Christmas Day in the morning.*
> *Three pretty maids were in those ships,*
> *In those ships, in those ships;*
> *Three pretty maids were in those ships,*
> *On Christmas Day in the morning.*
> *One could whistle and one could sing,*
> *And one could play the violin;*
> *Such joy there was at my wedding*
> *On Christmas Day in the morning.*

It is scarcely discreet to allow strange craft—especially strange craft with lovely lasses on board—to go roaming about the high seas at their own sweet will. So I made it my business to overhaul and search the holds of these three mysterious vessels. As I drew near, I saw nothing of the three pretty maids of whose personal charms and musical accomplishments the carol-singers were so enamored. Since sound travels easily across water, I listened intently on the off-chance that she of the thrush-like whistle, or she of the dulcet voice, or she whose magic touch could woo such sweetness from the violin, might at least be rehearsing at the moment. But no such luck was mine.

One thing, however, both impressed and alarmed me, especially in view of the fact that the lives of these three enchanting damsels depended on the safety of the ships now riding at anchor in the bay. I could not help noticing that all three vessels were very low down in the water. I was not surprised, therefore, when on closer investigation, I discovered that all three were shockingly and dangerously overloaded. Had I permitted them to put to sea in the condition in which I found them, they must inevitably have foundered in the first gale that smote them. But let me go into particulars.

I

The first of these ships—as trimly-built a little vessel as you could wish to see—was named the *Retrospect*. After exchanging compliments with the captain, he ordered the hold to be opened, and I found that the ship was laden with a cargo of Memories. Now memories are good things, and I shall say no single word—especially at Christmastime—in disparagement of the cargo of the *Retrospect*. At this season of the year, we all indulge in a riot of recollection and reminiscence. We sing the old songs; we play the old games; we tell the old stories; and we surround ourselves—in fact or in fancy—with the old familiar faces. We conjure up thoughts of old-time feasts and old-time frolics. In a word, we do all that is humanly possible to make the dead past live again.

As I glanced down into her cavernous hold, I saw at once that the *Retrospect* carried most valuable freight. Memories are precious store. It is well worth while to treasure up the sunshine of the days gone by, and to take it out for our warmth and illumination in times that are bleak and cheerless. In days when the world is treating us harshly, it is just as well to behave as the bees do, living in winter on the honey that we have stored in the long, luxurious summer hours. I always notice at the cricket ground that, whenever the play becomes provocative rather of soporific yawns than of excited yells, the grey and grizzled veterans seek sanctuary in a rainbow-tinted past and tell each other thrilling stories—some of them true—concerning the sensational exploits of the champions of the days of auld lang syne.

Excellent as all this is, it remains true that you can have too much even of a good thing. I saw at once that the *Retrospect* carried far too many memories. She was badly overloaded. Most of us remember too much. We may possibly forget a few things that we ought to remember; but we certainly remember thousands of things that we ought to forget. Christmastime is an ideal time for jettisoning superfluous cargo. There are ugly memories, bitter memories, filthy memories, irritating memories. The wretched things are as heavy as lead, yet utterly worthless. Why imperil both passengers and crew by carrying such dangerous stuff?

Many years ago I visited an old man on his deathbed. He was a man whom nobody liked—hard, sullen, taciturn and dour. If you met him on the street and wished him 'Good day,' he would keep his eyes straight in front of him, grunt sulkily and pass on. He lived in a tumbledown old hut away back in the bush; he spoke to nobody; and he made it perfectly plain that he wished nobody to speak to him. Even the children shunned him. Some said that he was a hermit; some that he was a woman-hater; some that he was a miser; some that he was a fugitive from justice, a man with a guilty secret.

But they were all wrong.

The simple truth was that, in his youth, a companion had done him a grievous injury. 'I'll remember it,' he had hissed in a gust of passionate resentment, 'I'll remember it to my dying day!' And he did. But when his dying day actually came, he realized that the rankling memory of that youthful wrong had soured and darkened his whole life.

'I've gone over it by myself every morning,' he moaned, as he lay gasping in his comfortless shanty, 'and I've thought of it every night. I've cursed him a hundred times each day. I see now,' he added brokenly, a suspicion of moisture glistening in his eye, 'I see now that my curses have eaten out my soul: they've been like gall on my tongue and gravel in my teeth. My hate has hurt nobody but myself. But God knows, it's turned my life into hell!'

It was true. The man at whom he had spat out his venomous maledictions, having done all that man could possibly do to atone for the suffering that he had thoughtlessly caused, had dismissed the matter from his mind a generation back. Upon *him* my gnarled old friend's bitterness had produced little or no effect. It was the man who cherished the sinister memory who suffered most. It shadowed his life; it lent a new terror to death: it expelled every trace of brightness and excluded every ray of hope: and at last, a grim and ghostly companion, it lay down with him in his cold and cheerless grave.

There is such a thing as the high art of forgetting. It is a divine art. The most astounding thing that the Bible tells us about God is that, remembering all that He wishes to remember, He forgets all that He wishes to forget. Even God declines to carry *everything* in His memory. He sternly refuses to harbor any recollection of the transgressions that He has once forgiven. *Their sins and iniquities will He remember no more.*

Convinced of this peril, the captain of the *Retrospect* ordered the crew to put ashore at least a third of the cargo. And, beyond the shadow of a doubt, the vessel will be all the better for the lightening of her load.

II

The second of these ships, the *Resolve*, was lying at anchor in the fairway, about a mile further downstream. As my boat came alongside, I could see that, with a fair wind blowing, the skipper was a trifle vexed at my arresting his progress in order to investigate. But he soon recovered, and we parted the best of friends. As soon as he produced the ship's papers, I saw that she was carrying a load of Good Resolutions. It is a very useful cargo, but it must be very carefully handled. Like fruit in cool store, it has to be kept at just the right temperature, or it quickly perishes. I am told that, of this line of goods, the proportion that reaches its ultimate destination in good condition is pitifully small. That may have accounted for the captain's anxiety to get to sea as speedily as possible. But it would never have done. If all the ships carrying good resolutions are loaded as the *Resolve* was loaded, I am not surprised that the cargo perishes on the journey. The things were packed like sardines: there were far too many of them.

It is absurd to overload the ship as the *Resolve* was overloaded. I ordered out the entire crew and told them to jettison the cargo until the Plimsoll line was clearly visible. The captain, recognizing the peril in which he had been placed, quite recovered from the annoyance that he had felt at my interference. As my boat pulled away from the sides of the *Resolve*, I felt a little remorseful at hearing the splash, splash, splash, as one Good Resolution after another was dropped into the waves; but I comforted myself with the reflection that it was better that a few should be lost in the harbor than that all should perish in mid-ocean. And so, with a cheery wave to the skipper, I came away.

III

In a cozy comer of the deck of the *Good Hope,* I espied a violin case. That was as near as I got to personal contact with the young ladies immortalized in the carol. As soon as the mate—the captain had gone ashore—told me of the freight he had on board, I saw that, as in the other cases, the *Good Hope* was badly overloaded. She had a cargo of Good Wishes. But dear me, she had enough of them to satisfy a transatlantic liner! And such tremendous wishes, too! The wonder was that the men had been able to pack such enormous commodities in the hold of so small a ship. We are all clever at wishing—or think that we are! But we badly overdo it. We indulge in blind wishes, ignorant wishes, thoughtless wishes.

We frequently wish for ourselves, and for others, the most ridiculous things, without giving a moment's consideration to the question as to whether life would be really enriched if the flippant wish were granted. Presumably we have never heard the story of King Midas, who wished that everything he touched might be turned to gold, and found himself cursed by the granting of his desire. The Japanese have a story of a man whose every wish was gratified, and, after a long cycle of changes and transfigurations, he finished up, to his infinite relief, in the condition from which he originally set out.

Towards the end of the New Testament there is a charming little private letter, written by the most lovable guest of the Bible to the most lovable host of the Bible. In such a letter, written by one old friend to another, we should naturally expect a fond and fervent wish, and we are not disappointed.

Beloved, says John, in opening his heart to Gaius,
I wish above all things that thou mayest prosper and
be in health even as thy soul prospereth!

That exquisite fragment should be examined under a microscope. It is a perfect specimen of the high art of wise wishing.

But I am forgetting all about the *Good Hope*. The mate asked me to take no drastic action until the captain returned, so we sat down on some bales of cargo to wait for him. He turned out to be a jolly-looking old fellow, rubicund and weather-beaten. He came on board whistling a jaunty air. As soon as I mentioned the matter, he agreed that the *Good Hope* was seriously overloaded, and at once set the crew to work to lighten her. I wished him and the mate a pleasant trip and returned to my boat. By the time I reached home, all three vessels were under a fine spread of canvas and were giving every promise of safe and prosperous voyages.

HOW CHRISTMAS CAME TO ROARING CAMP

IT MAY OR MAY NOT HAVE HAPPENED in December; Bret Harte does not say, and it certainly does not matter, for whether it happened in April or September or December, it was Christmastime in Roaring Camp. It is always Christmastime when a little child is born; the angels sing their song in somebody's sky, and heaven fills the atmosphere of somebody's home with its *Gloria in Excelsis*—its message of peace on earth and goodwill among men.

I

It was certainly Christmastime in Roaring Camp. Peace and goodwill were unknown at Roaring Camp until that little babe was born. Even among the mining camps of the lawless West, Roaring Camp had a sinister and unenviable notoriety. When men differed in opinion over their cards, and, to settle the dispute, shot each other dead on the spot, the gamblers at the neighboring tables merely nodded and calmly went on with their games. To die a natural death at Roaring Camp was to die at the pistol's point.

There was just one woman there—poor Cherokee Sal—and, as Bret Harte says on the first page of the story, the less said of her, the better. And anyhow, she dies, and dies at the beginning of the tale. Stumpy, who in earlier and better days, had been a medical student or something of the sort, did his best for her. He managed to save the baby, but the plight of poor Sal was beyond his skill.

The baby belonged to the Camp, and the Camp resolved to do its duty bravely. The baby was lying on some rags in a box. The character of the box is not recorded; it wasn't a soap box—soap was a negligible quantity at Roaring Camp. But everybody felt that the box wouldn't do; so a man was sent eighty miles on a mule to get a rosewood cradle, the best that money could buy. The cradle was brought; but then the rags seemed out of place, and the messenger had to return to Sacramento for the daintiest and softest lace and filigree-work and frills, to be bought regardless of cost. But when the pink little baby, lying amidst its froth of snowy white-work in the rosewood cradle, took his place in the middle of the room, the men noticed with dismay a thing that they had never noticed before: the floor was positively filthy! And when they had scrubbed the floor, as only horny-handed miners could scrub it, and made it almost as clean as on the day on which the boards were first laid, they made a new discovery. For they saw that, in order to match the floor and the rosewood cradle and the lace-work and the baby, the walls would have to be cleaned and the ceiling whitewashed, and the windows mended and draped with curtains!

Moreover, there had to be long periods of quiet, to allow the baby to sleep, and so the quality that had given the Camp its name departed from it. The men took the rosewood cradle out to the mines on the fine days; but the mining area was a dusty, dreary place; so, to please the baby's eye, they planted brightly-colored flowers round the spot where the cradle stood; they had, of course, to plant them in some kind of order and with some design; and so the very mines became a garden. The men noticed, too, that some of the stones that they turned up with their picks had a certain brightness and beauty; they found themselves putting aside glittering bits of quartz, prettily-colored pebbles and flakes of mica as playthings for the baby! Best of all, a change came over the appearance of the men themselves. Up at Tuttle's Store, the astute proprietor, seeing which way the wind was blowing down at the camp, placed mirrors about the apartment in which the men lounged and chatted and smoked. And soon there was an extraordinary demand for soap and shaving materials, collars, ties, and even suits of clothes. The baby transformed everything!

II

Which things are an allegory—a Christmas allegory. The world itself was Roaring Camp two thousand years ago. As Matthew Arnold says in *Obermann*:

> *On that hard pagan world disgust*
> *And secret loathing fell:*
> *Deep weariness and sated lust*
> *Made human life a hell,*

Man—every man—was either a slave-owner or a slave, either a pitiless tyrant or a cringing victim. Womanhood was debased and dishonored. Childhood was destitute of sanctity; children, unwanted, were strangled or drowned; there was nothing to prevent it: nobody cared.

Then a little Child was born at Bethlehem. In the presence of that little Child, men saw, as they had never seen before, that the world needed tidying-up. The cry of the slave would not harmonize with the song of the angels, so slavery had to go. The degradation of womanhood was put to shame by the human grace and divine glory of the Virgin Mother. A halo fell upon the brows of motherhood. The drudge was lifted from the dust at the feet of her lord and seated by his side, his helpmeet, his companion, his queen. And, ever since that little Babe was born, childhood has been treated as a sacred thing. The deeply-entrenched evils of antiquity have been swept away. And the deeply-entrenched evils of modernity are doomed. As the little Child of Bethlehem asserts His authority over the hearts of men, the smudges that still disfigure our civilization must vanish one by one. The bitterness of our industrial strife; the vices of our social life; the menace of the liquor evil; the horrors, crimes, and agonies of war—all these must yield to His sublime authority. As surely as the Babe of Bethlehem is the Son of God, the regeneration of Roaring Camp must be carried to completion.

III

And the same is true of the individual soul. What is it that Angelus Silesius sings?

> *Though Christ a thousand times*
> *In Bethlehem be born.*
> *If He's not born in thee*
> *Thy soul is all forlorn.*

That is the point. The Christ-child is born afresh; and the heart is the inn; and the angels sing again as they sang in the fields of Bethlehem; and shepherds and sages come once more to see the wonder that has come to pass. And, in that same soul, all the miracles are repeated; blindness vanishes; song visits dumb lips;

deafness yields to the hearing of unutterable things; leprosy departs and death trembles into life. That is the message of Christmas, and every Christmas as it comes lends to that message a new meaning and a new music.

ALOES

A Christmas Wooing

Christmas in the Studio

A Little Chap in Knickerbockers

A Clouded Christmas

A CHRISTMAS WOOING

THE HUGE RATA TREE IS A MASS of gorgeous crimson; and from the seclusion of its branches the sweet and liquid notes of the tui are floating down the steep and graceful hillside. The bird's only auditors are the two Maori girls reclining on the grass a hundred yards away.

You can see at a glance that they are sisters, perhaps twin sisters. Waitawi and Omimi are about seventeen, although, following the fashion of their swarthy race, they have matured prematurely, so that their rich, ripe womanhood would convey to European eyes the impression that they are several years older than the facts would warrant.

All this is preeminently true of Omimi. Wrapped in her native shawl, so cunningly compounded of flax and feathers, she sits on the grass beside her prostrate sister. Behind them, guarded by the flaming rata in whose branches the tui sings, stands their hut, stoutly constructed, ornately carved, elaborately adorned, thatched with raupo and carpeted with mats of many curious designs.

Waitawi loves to be brought out on to the open hillside. Here, by simply turning her head, she can survey the glorious panorama that unrolls itself with such magnificence and charm around her. With the snowcapped mountains in the background, and the blue bay far below, Waitawi likes to watch the restless waves churning themselves into foam against the jagged cliffs; and, even in their ceaseless moaning, she finds a music that lulls her mind and strangely soothes her pain.

I

For Waitawi has been hurt. Although she so closely resembles her more active sister, it is clear that her features are slightly thinner, her face a trifle drawn. A month or two ago Waitawi was even stronger, nimbler and more agile than Omimi. Indeed, it was because her sinews were so supple, and her foot so fleet, that she undertook the hazardous mission that involved her in such serious injury.

The father of the girls had set out with a numerous band of tattooed warriors, fully armed, who had undertaken to wreak vengeance on the chiefs of Tippahee for having savagely attacked the natives of the Bay of Islands. They had reason to believe that the enemy was lurking on the opposite side of the bay, and, in that confidence, they set out to march round the sandy shores to destroy them. A little later, however, Omimi and Waitawi discovered that their men-folk had been misinformed; and, fearful lest their father should walk into a Tippahee trap, they resolved at any cost to warn him.

'I will go,' exlaimed Waitawi, stimulated to unwonted vigor by her father's peril. 'I can run, and I can climb, and I can jump, and I can swim! I will reach him before the moon has risen over the hut, and by daylight I will be back again!' And, almost before Omimi had realized what had happened, her sprightly sister had disappeared.

Long before the pale moonbeams could have risen over the hut, Waitawi came upon the camp. But as soon as she approached, she made a discovery that froze her blood with terror. These were the men of Tippahee! Like a frightened deer, she dashed off in the only direction that was open to her. Chased by the startled tribesmen, she headed straight for the sea. Before her was a sheer precipice fifty feet deep. She rushed to the edge and dived, leaving her pursuers gazing vacantly into the abyss into which she had vanished.

Exactly what happened she never knew. She found herself in the swirling water, with limbs that throbbed with pain. Making a desperate effort, she swam round the cliff, crept up the beach, and, in agony, crawled home. She knew that her wound was mortal. The sands in the hourglass soon ran out. One evening the sisters had been watching the last sunset that Waitawi was ever to see.

When the saffron and the turquoise of the clouds had died into a drab slate-grey, and first one star and then another lit up the vault above them, Waitawi turned to her sister with grave and pleading eyes, and asked a question that Omimi never forgot.

'What is it,' she entreated, 'that the stars are always singing? Lying here at night, I listen to their song; but cannot catch the words. What is it that they sing?'

Omimi could not answer, so she remained silent. And in that long stillness that ensued, Waitawi's eyes closed for ever.

II

A few years later Omimi, grown to full and beautiful womanhood, was standing near the hut with a tall young Maori, Tuatini by name, who had enjoyed an amazing and almost incredible adventure. In a dare-devil moment he had boarded a whaling ship lying in the bay, and had sailed away with the white men.

After knocking about the world, he had begun to cherish homeward thoughts, and had engaged himself on the convict ship *William*, bound for Sydney.

On that same ship the Rev. Samuel Marsden was travelling to Australia to take up his appointment as chaplain to the new settlement. Pacing the quarterdeck one day, Mr. Marsden was astonished at beholding in the forecastle a youth with a tawny skin.

From that moment the two felt powerfully attracted to each other. The stalwart young Maori, with his tall and handsome frame, his fine, open countenance, and his keen, dark eyes, made a magnetic and resistless appeal to the chaplain's interest and sympathy.

Tuatini was Mr. Marsden's first convert. When they parted in Sydney, Tuatini begged Mr. Marsden to visit New Zealand, and to tell his people the wonderful things that he had unfolded to him. The chaplain promised, if possible, to do so; but urged Tuatini, in the meantime, to regard himself as the pioneer evangelist of his own people.

III

Tuatini did his best. One of the first to attend sympathetically to his sensational story was Omimi, who since her sister's death had spent much time in solitary excursions in the bush, pondering deeply on the mystery of things unseen. But the eagerness

that Omimi displayed was shared by few. The
natives laughed derisively as Tuatini described the
things he had seen in the land of the white men.

He told them how the white man sowed his crop
and ground his corn and made his bread. They rose
in derisive laughter and refused to believe a word of
it. But Tuatini had prudently provided himself with a
tiny bag of wheat and a coffee mill. The sceptical Maoris
stood around the little plot on the hillside while Tuatini
prepared his soil and sowed his seed. They nudged
each other, tapped their foreheads and exchanged
significant glances. Much travel, they thought, had
wrecked poor Tuatini's brain or brought him under
the witchery of an evil spirit. But when there appeared
first the blade and then the ear and then the full corn
in the ear, their countenances changed. They crowded
round and watched Tuatini grind his corn in the coffee
mill. They ate, with wonder, of the bread which, with
Omimi's assistance, he made from the snowy flour. For
a while they listened with more respect to that still more
wonderful story of which Tuatini loved to speak. But
the young evangelist spoiled it all by telling one wildly
impossible tale which the tribesmen could never believe.
Over the sea, he said, the white man had an animal a
thousand times as big as a rat, and the white man sat
upon its back and made it bear him; and harnessed
it to his heavy burdens and made it drag them. The
scornful natives awoke the echoes of the hills with their

boisterous laughter as they derided this preposterous narrative. It was useless for Tuatini to approach more serious and momentous themes; they simply declined to listen. And even the gentle Omimi suspected that Tuatini was trading upon her credulity. And thus the young missionary found himself under a cloud of scepticism, and his work made little progress. 'Oh,' he sighed as he sat of an evening looking with hungry eyes across the blue, blue sea, 'if only Mr. Marsden would come! If Mr. Marsden would only come!'

And, after weary years of waiting, Mr. Marsden purchased a ship and came! And, fortunately, he brought his horse with him. As the Maoris watched the white man riding the powerful animal along the sands and up the slope, they remembered Tuatini's words and looked at each other in speechless amazement. The incident forcefully inclined their minds to listen attentively to all that Tuatini's foreign friend might say. As for Tuatini himself, he was in transports of delight. It happened to be Christmas Eve, and no man ever spent a happier Christmastime than Tuatini spent in 1814. He insisted that Mr. Marsden must address his countrymen on Christmas afternoon. It chanced to be a Sunday. How proudly Tuatini made all the preliminary arrangements, prepared the pulpit and undertook the duties of interpreter!

A massive stone cross still marks the lovely spot on which that service—the first ever conducted in New

Zealand—was held. It was a glorious midsummer day: the sea shimmering in the clear sunshine: the sky a cloudless blue. When Mr. Marsden rose, the silence was broken only by the rhythmic surge of the waves on the crescent beach below. The Maoris had gathered from all the *pas* in the vicinity. Among them Mr. Marsden was amused to notice three scarred old chiefs, attired in all the glory of some old uniforms which had found their way out from England. Swords dangled by their sides, and they held native switches in their hands. 'I stood up,' says Mr. Marsden, 'and began by singing the Old Hundredth Psalm, while my soul melted within me as I looked round at the people, most of whom were cannibals. It was Christmas Day, and my text was in every way appropriate to the situation. It was the message of the angel to the shepherds of Bethlehem,

"Behold I bring you glad tidings of great joy!" '

IV

That Christmas Day was a beginning of days for New Zealand: it was the first chapter in the nation's history. And it was a beginning of days for Omimi and Tuatini. For that evening, as the sunset was transforming the bay into a sheen of purple and gold, they were married by

Mr. Marsden. And as, a little later, they watched the stars stud the cloudless sky, Omimi said that, after hearing all that Mr. Marsden had said about the Shepherds in the Fields and about the Star of Bethlehem, she thought she knew the words of the mystical song about which Waitawi had so wistfully inquired. Omimi was satisfied—perfectly satisfied and radiantly happy. And when, next morning, the sunlight came streaming through the entrance of the hut, the tui was again singing blithely in the rata tree above them.

CHRISTMAS IN THE STUDIO

IT WAS THE NIGHT BEFORE CHRISTMAS in the year 1769. Although it had been snowing all day and was snowing still, a jovial air pervaded the solemn old city of Stuttgart. In most of the windows the blinds were undrawn, that every passerby might admire the Christmas tree and the colorful decorations.

Among the crazy little streets converging on the Schloss-Platz, three boys were keeping themselves warm by playing hide-and-seek and chasing one another over the frozen pavements. Suddenly, in dashing round a dark corner, one of them collided violently with an elderly gentleman whose arms were laden with parcels of every shape and size.

'*Donner und blitzen,* you young Clumsy-boots!' exclaimed the startled greybeard as, deprived of breath, he steadied himself against the wall.

'Forgive me, sir,' replied the frightened boy as he gathered the scattered packages and offered to help carry them home.

'Who are you! What's your name?' asked the old man, who secretly liked the look of the youngster when, in the dim light of the street lamp, the open countenance with its shock of fair hair and its pale blue eyes was eagerly raised to his own.

'My name, sir, is Johann Dannecker, and my father works at the Palace stables.' Walking along through the whirling snow, the good man asked a hundred questions as to the lad's education and prospects. Some of his friends, Johann explained, wished him to be a professional dancer; but he himself wanted to be a soldier.

'Well, listen to me,' the grave and reverend senior entreated earnestly as he took farewell of his strangely-met companion. 'Make up your mind that, whatever you become, you'll do something before you die for which the world will always bless you!' Johann Dannecker never saw the old man again; but he never forgot that parting injunction.

I

While still in his teens, Johann conceived the idea that he had not long to live, but, with a thought of the experience that came to him on that memorable Christmas Eve, he vowed that he would give the world a masterpiece that would be treasured forever. It was for this reason that, instead of becoming a dancer or a warrior, he became a sculptor; he fancied that a noble statue stood a better chance of living through the ages than any other work of which human hands were capable. Setting to work early, he quickly achieved fame.

His *Mars*, his *Ceres*, his *Bacchus*, his *Sappho*, his *Hector*, his *Psyche*, and his *Ariadne* are still among the adornments of the great European capitals. But Dannecker was not satisfied. None of these impressed him as bearing the stamp of immortality; he therefore gave himself to contemplation—and to prayer. One evening, as he pondered his New Testament, he came upon this fragment of a primitive hymn;

> *Without controversy great*
> *Is the mystery of godliness;*
> *God was manifest in the flesh,*
> *He was justified in the Spirit;*
> *He was seen of Angels;*
> *He was preached unto the Gentiles;*
> *He was believed on in the world,*
> *He was received up into glory.*

Fascinated, he read the lines again and again. If only he could catch their spirit and express it in eloquent marble! He would try! He prayed for grace and guidance; his entire personality and genius were sublimely consecrated to the exalted task.

II

He completed at length his first cast of his statue of the
Divine Christ. He invited a group of children to visit his
studio and to inspect his work. They gazed admiringly
at the stately figure, and then one boy exclaimed: 'He
must have been a very great man.' Dannecker was
bitterly disappointed. The impression of greatness was
not the impression that he had aspired to convey. He
thanked the children and dismissed them.

Having set to work afresh and completed his
second cast, he sent for a fresh group of children to
visit him. This time they smiled appreciatively and felt
magnetically drawn to the lovely figure on the pedestal.
It was a girl who broke the silence. 'He must have been
a very good man!' she exclaimed. Dannecker was less
displeased than before; but he was by no means satisfied.
He decided to make a third attempt.

III

This final cast having been completed, he again sent for
a batch of children. Garbed in his long white overalls,
he scrutinized their faces as they entered the studio.
This time, to his secret delight, the boys snatched off

their caps as they caught sight of the statue, while one of the girls fell on her knees. Dannecker felt that at last he had expressed the adoration that was in his heart. He completed his work; and the statue—one of the most famous in the world—is, to this day, the pride of his native city of Stuttgart.

While Europe was still ringing with his fame, Napoleon summoned Dannecker to Paris. 'You must,' said the Emperor, 'make me a statue of Venus for the Louvre.' 'Sire,' replied the sculptor, 'the man who, receiving a divine vision, makes it the theme of his loftiest achievement, would commit an unspeakable sacrilege if he were then to devote his powers to the carving of a pagan goddess. My art has been consecrated by my work!' It was said of him that the concentration and intensity with which he applied himself to his statue of the *Christ* undermined his health, but transfigured his personality.

The story is worth recalling whenever the Christmas bells are ringing.

A LITTLE CHAP IN KNICKERBOCKERS

'MURDER! MURDER! MURDER!'

It was Christmas night. The feasts and frolics of the great day were over. The walls were festooned with colored streamers; the pictures were hung with ivy and holly; the floor was littered with the tattered remnants of tissue paper headgear—crowns and miters and helmets. The children, flushed and excited, had fought the sandman bravely; but had been forced at last to capitulate, and, yawning in spite of themselves, had stolen off to bed. I slipped into the study to arrange one or two papers before retiring. Yielding to the seductions of my big armchair and an alluring magazine, I must have dozed.

I

'Help! Help! Help!' I heard somebody cry.

Looking round in amazement, I quickly recognized that the muffled sounds were proceeding from the Waste Paper Basket.

'What on earth can be the matter?' I asked myself half-audibly as, bending over that useful asylum for tattered envelopes and superannuated circulars, I commenced to rummage among its heterogenous contents. I soon discovered that the commotion was being created by a plain little, cheap little, common little Christmas card, a crude representation of a red-robed Santa Claus driving his toy-laden sledge through deep snow, while, across the corner of the card, in inartistic tinseled letters that glistened under the electric light, appeared the greeting: *A Merry Christmas!*

'The very idea!' exclaimed the crumpled card as I gently disentangled it from the wrappings of a bar of chocolate and the remnants of an exploded bon-bon, 'the very idea of murdering the Spirit of Christmas in this way! And on Christmas Day of all days!'

I impotently confessed my bewilderment. 'And anyhow,' I added, 'no harm's done! Here you are, safe and sound, very little the worse for having spent the evening in the basket! You ought to be thankful that you were not thrown into the fire. If it had been in England, where Christmas comes at midwinter instead of midsummer, that's what would have happened to you!'

'You miss the whole point!' retorted the indignant card. 'You know as well as I do that you only throw into the Waste Paper Basket the things for which you feel an utter contempt. If a letter is very confidential or very compromising, you toss it into the flames and watch it blaze; and you pay an unconscious tribute to its importance by destroying it so carefully. Or, if a letter fills your heart with pride, or strikes you as being of value for future reference, you file it or docket it or consign it to a drawer or a pigeonhole. But the things that you despise, the things that are in your way, the things that are a bore and a nuisance to you, you fling disdainfully into the Waste Paper Basket! You don't care who sees them or what becomes of them! And that's how you treated *me!* You wouldn't have behaved like that towards a Christmas card when you were a little chap in knickerbockers! It's because you have slain the romance of Christmas in your soul that you wanted me out of your way!'

II

Startled, out of my slumber by this stinging rebuke, I looked around me. All was quiet. The Waste Paper Basket showed no signs of the disturbance that I seemed to have witnessed. The room was chilly and lonely; so, imitating the children—whom it is always good to imitate at Christmastime—I too, crept off to bed. But a guilty feeling was upon me.

I remembered many things that seemed to indicate that the crumpled card had spoken justly. I remembered, for example, my conversation on the tram with poor old Stephen Griggs. It was about a week before Christmas: the car was crowded with people carrying parcels: and everybody was wishing everybody else the compliments of the season.

'I suppose Christmas is all very well,' he muttered as, after standing for some time, I at length found a vacant seat beside him; 'it seems to please some people; but, for my part, I'm mighty glad when it's all over! You've got to rack your brains to think of all the people to whom you ought to send presents or cards, and then there's the worry of choosing the wretched things! And see how it upsets business! Why, you don't get straight again for a week or two afterwards! And besides,' he added, looking dreadfully serious, 'it's horribly expensive, and I really believe it gets more expensive every year!'

In rising to leave the car at my stopping-place, I fear that, for courtesy's sake, I feebly murmured some commonplace of sympathy or agreement; but my subsequent experience with the Waste Paper Basket has shown me what I ought to have done.

'Cheer up, old friend!' I should have said, slapping him on the shoulder as I bade him Goodbye. 'Don't make a worry of it! Just send your cards and your presents to the people to whom you would really like to send them: the others won't break their hearts at being left out! And if the expense is troubling you, why, instead of sending anything costly, just sit down and write a cheery, chatty letter—a letter that will keep you smiling all the time you're writing it and that will keep them chuckling all the time they're reading it. And, instead of puzzling about presents for people whose wants you don't know, just call in and spend a rollicking half-hour with them! Tell them the best stories you've heard this year! Have a romp with the children—perhaps give them some sweets! Then grip them all by the hand, pour out your good wishes, and come away! Do you remember,' I should have added, anticipating the phraseology of the crumpled card, 'do you remember the jolly old Christmases that you used to spend when you were a little chap in knickerbockers? Well, have a Christmas like that this year! So long!'

III

It is a thousand pities that I did not address poor old Stephen in this way. It would have generated in his clouded soul the makings of a truly merry Christmas. 'A little chap in knickerbockers!' he would have mused; and the light of old-time Christmases would have shone in his eyes, and the laughter of old-time Christmases would have rung in his ears. In pleasing fancy he would have seen once more the old familiar faces in their old familiar places: he would have conjured up the vision of bulging stockings, blazing snapdragons and a many-candied Christmas tree! In the dusty mirror of his withered heart he would have seen again the flushed cheeks and sparkling eyes of the dainty little sweetheart whom, when she was eight and he was ten, he kissed beneath the mistletoe! And, swept off his feet by the carefree spirit of those far-off frolics, he would have been a boy—a knickerbockered boy—again!

But it was too late! I could not go back to my old friend on the tram; and, anyway, Christmas was over! The crumpled card could do nothing to invest with gaiety that shadowed festival. No magic can recall the past. But my mind turned, in that last moment of the day, to the Christmases unborn. By hook or by crook, I said to myself, we must recapture for those coming Christmases the enchanted spirit of childhood! It is the golden key that alone can unlock the shining gates of Fairyland! And, reflecting thus, I once more fell asleep and once more dreamed!

I dreamed that we were all boys and girls again. And, by that subtle magnetism that always draws a child to the spot where happy children play, I thought that the Child of Bethlehem joined our joyous party; and the angels sang their *Gloria in Excelsis* in the Yuletide air. And, when the fun was at its height, those choicest and most genial of Christmas guests—*Peace-on-Earth* and *Goodwill-toward-Men*—took the armchairs on either side of the hearth and breathed their smiling benedictions on the merry company.

A CLOUDED CHRISTMAS

IT IS AN INFINITE COMFORT TO us ordinary pulpiteers to know that even an Archbishop may sometimes have a bad time! And, on the occasion of which I write, the poor Prelate must have had a very bad time indeed. For—tell it not in Gath, publish it not in the streets of Askelon!—none of his hearers knew what he had been talking about! They could make neither head nor tail of it! 'I have not been able to find one man yet who could discover what it was about,' wrote one of his auditors to a friend. It is certainly most humiliating when our congregations go home and pen such letters for posterity to chuckle over.

And yet the ability of the preacher at this particular service, and the intelligence of his hearers, are alike beyond question. For the preacher was the famous Richard Chenevix Trench, D.D., Professor of Theology at King's College, Dean of Westminster and Archbishop of Dublin. The sermon was preached in the classical atmosphere of Cambridge University, principally to students and undergraduates. The theme was the Incarnation—'*the Word was made flesh.*' And the young fellow who wrote the plaintive epistle from which I have quoted was Alfred Ainger, afterwards a distinguished literateur and Master of the Temple. He could make nothing of it. 'The sermon, I am sorry to say, was universally disappointing. I have not been able to find one man yet who could discover what it was about. It is needless to say *I* could not. He chose, too, one of the grandest and most profound texts in the New Testament. He talked a great deal about St. Augustine, but any more I cannot tell you.'

Now Christmas is once more knocking at our doors, and many of us, in a few days, will find ourselves preaching on this self-same theme. And we have a wholesome horror of sending our hearers home in the same fearful perplexity. 'What on earth was the minister talking about. All the cards and the carols, the fun and the frolic, the pastimes and the picnics will be turned into dust and ashes, into gall and wormwood, into vanity and vexation of spirit to the poor preacher who suspects that his Christmas congregation returned home in such a mood. His Christmas dinner will almost choke him. There will be no merry Christmas for *him!*

But let no minister be terrified or intimidated by the Archbishop's unhappy experience. His 'bad time' may help us to enjoy a good one. We must take his text, and wrestle with it bravely. It is just the message for Christmas. There is none like it. 'Christmas approaches!' writes James Smetham in his *Journal*. 'Christmas approaches, a charmed time for me. I hear its music afar off—the song of the angels, the pealing of the bells, but most of all, the divine song from out the central glory.' And this divine sentence from the lips of the King will come up every hour with wondrous depth and meaning. '*The Word was made flesh* and dwelt among us.' Yes, it is the ideal Christmas greeting. There is certainly depth and mystery; but there is humanness and tenderness as well.

I

No man has come within sight of elucidating the stately mystery of Chrismastime until he discovers that, in the birth of the Babe in the manger, God wrote His own divine autobiography. Bethlehem is a superb masterpiece of celestial self-revelation. Almighty God gave us His eternal life-story, inscribed, not with pen and ink, but with flesh and blood.

In contemplating the redemption of the world, God was confronted by a problem worthy of his infinite genius! It is said of Huber, the great Swiss naturalist, that, as a boy, he one day stood with his mother beside an anthill. The ants were scurrying everywhere in obvious agitation. 'They're afraid of me!' the boy remarked to his mother. 'But,' she replied, 'you wouldn't hurt them; you are so fond of them!' 'Yes,' answered the boy, 'but how can I let the ants know that I'm so fond of them—

except by becoming an ant?' There you have the problem
in a cameo. How could Almighty God let men know that
He was so fond of them—*except by becoming a man?*
And it is the supreme triumph of divine ingenuity that
He actually compassed that end.

The Word that He ached to speak became flesh.
Wren expressed himself in granite; Turner expressed
himself in oils; Michelangelo expressed himself in
marble; Shakespeare expressed himself in ink; but God
selected *flesh* as the ideal vehicle for self-expression.

The Word was made flesh! The only quality with
which God had endowed man, and which He did not
Himself possess, was—flesh. He therefore selected the
hallmark of man's humanity as the supreme vehicle for
the revelation of His love.

Flesh! There is nothing so eloquent. When the
soul most aches for expression, one's speech becomes
strangely broken and incoherent. In the crises of life we
express ourselves, not in stately diction and exquisitely
balanced sentences, but in the awkwardness of the
limbs, in the confusion of the face and in a welter of
embarrassment. The twitching of the lips; the pallor
of the countenance; the crimsoning of the cheeks;
the moistening of the eyes—these telltale signals are
incomparably more eloquent and incalculably more
revealing than any mere words could possibly be. For
they are flesh; and flesh is the ideal medium for self-
expression. That is why God chose it.

II

We never understand words until they are '*made flesh.*' Let me illustrate my meaning. Here is a bonny little fellow of six, with sunny face and a glorious shock of golden hair. His father hands him his first spelling book, with the alphabet on the front page, and little two-letter monosyllables following. But he can make nothing of it. Then his mother sits beside him, slips her arm round his shoulders, gently explains the mysterious hieroglyphics, and when, in the person of his mother, the words become flesh, comprehension dawns upon him.

Ten years later he is a perfect bookworm. He reads every adventure story that he can lay his hands on. But again he is mystified. 'Mother,' he says, 'why, in each of these books, is there one of those silly love-stories?' He is hopelessly out of his depth.

But ten years later still! The greatest word in the language—the word that so bewildered him in his earlier travel stories—the word 'love'—is made flesh to him in the charming person of a pretty girl. And thus exquisitely incarnated, he once more understands.

We humans understand nothing until it is made flesh. That is why Jesus came. The Word *was made flesh*— soft flesh, warm flesh, live flesh that throbbed and felt and developed and matured, as all sound and healthy flesh will. And so there grew up, little by little, line upon line, the sweetest idyll in the language—the life of Jesus. And Jesus is God; He is the pronunciation of the unpronounceable Word! I may look upon Him at any stage of His fleshly development—a Babe at Bethlehem, a Boy at Nazareth, a Youth at the Carpenter's Bench, a Man at Galilee—and, under whatever phase I behold him, I say to myself: 'Almighty God! Almighty God!' The Word, having been made flesh, has become intelligible and comprehensible at last! God reveals Himself in the beauty and the wonder of the universe; but a million universes would not tell me what Jesus tells me, for, in Jesus, *the Word was made flesh!* God reveals Himself in prophet and psalmist and apostle and sage; but a million Bibles would not tell me what Jesus tells me, for, in Jesus, *the Word was made flesh!*

III

The longer we live, and the more Christmases we spend, the greater grows the glory of the Incarnation. The Manger becomes a casket in which all the jewels of divine revelation glitter with increasing luster. A little Baby throws out its arms and cries; and, in its outstretched arms and piteous cry, we have a cameo of Calvary. For Golgotha is implicit in Bethlehem; the redemption of the world is wrapped in swaddling clothes; the conquest of the ages has begun! That is the subtle and sublime significance of Christmastime; and, come Christmas when it may—in the snow-white robes of wintertime, as it comes to the peoples of the northern world, or in the golden splendor of high summertime, as it comes to us beneath these Australian skies—it will always and everywhere awaken a responsive chord in hearts that are restless and ill at ease until they have heard the divine Word simply and clearly enunciated at Bethlehem.

CASSIA

A Christmas Crime

Brown Paper and String

The Invisible Children

The Lost Chronicles of Sufi-Abbas

A CHRISTMAS CRIME

THIS IS THE STORY, NOT OF a rapturous Christmas-time, nor of a melodious Christmas chime, nor of a lyrical Christmas rhyme, but of a most romantic Christmas crime.

I

'Have you moved the goose from the wood-shed?'

We were just sitting down to breakfast on Christmas Eve when our hostess entered the room, and, focusing an anxious scrutiny upon her husband's face, propounded this most unexpected and most disconcerting question.

Amidst tumultuous excitement, the handsome and appetizing bird had, the previous evening, arrived in a crate from an up-country farm. A letter received earlier in the week had apprised the family of its dispatch, and, from that hour, the three boys—Jack, Ron and Keith—had haunted the railway station like uneasy spirits. Immediately upon the arrival of a train, from whatever direction, they plied the harassed porters with eager enquiries concerning the feverishly expected goose.

And when at last, to the infinite relief of the officials, the package duly appeared, the trio dashed off home at breakneck speed to report the sensational arrival. In a few moments their father drove them back to the station in the car, and the goose was borne triumphantly home. The family having resolved, after a solemn conclave, to defer the execution until the morning, the traveler was released from its crate and imprisoned in the woodshed for the night.

This all happened during our stay at The Pines at Oterakani in New Zealand. As everybody in that romantic neighborhood knows, the Humes are most delightful people. Frederick Hume was the leading solicitor in the town; at the time of our visit he was Mayor of the municipality and has since represented the district in Parliament. He was, moreover, an elder of the Presbyterian Church and a natural leader in all the best movements among the people. Tall, dark and handsome, with fine eyes, clean, athletic figure and strikingly-molded face, he somehow impressed everybody with the feeling that he was in complete control of the situation, whatever that situation might happen to be. His very presence commanded confidence and respect, and his wife exquisitely matched his charm. The Pines, a massive and substantial building standing well back from the road and picturesquely surrounded by graceful lawns and flowering shrubs, is easily the most striking and beautiful home in that part of New Zealand. It is scarcely surprising, therefore, that the fortnight during which we luxuriated in its hospitality is treasured in our memories as one of the choicest and most notable of life's experiences.

II

The three boys—the eldest eleven, the youngest seven—stared at each other in blank astonishment. For them the earth had suddenly ceased to revolve. The goose not in the woodshed! It was of no use proceeding with breakfast: appetites were in ruins. Like a jury in an important case, we adjourned to inspect the scene of the tragedy. Only two theories were admissible; the goose had somehow escaped of its own accord or it had been maliciously stolen. As, with the shed shut up, the only avenues of escape appeared to be the chinks between the boards and the crack round the door, the first of these theories commanded scant support.

Driven perforce to the alternative conclusion, the boys consulted their legal adviser as to the maximum penalty that could be imposed on a thief who stole a goose on Christmas Eve. They themselves cherished a profound conviction that, for their personal delectation, the culprit should be hanged within sight of their windows as they sat at their gooseless dinner on Christmas Day. Their father, however, foresaw legal difficulties that might deprive them of this alluring entertainment.

Following upon our early-morning disturbance, we resumed our seats at the breakfast table, and, in spite of everything, did fair justice to the meal. There was, of course, but one topic of conversation. For a while the discussion concerned itself exclusively with the discovery, arrest and punishment of the thief; but, after many possible lines of action had been suggested and dismissed, Mr. Hume advised his sons to leave that aspect of the matter in expert hands.

'I shall be seeing Superintendent Lewis this morning,' he explained, 'and I'll mention the matter to him. If anything can be done, you may depend upon it the police will do it.'

'Well, then,' declared Ron, 'I'm going to have a good search! The goose may have got out: you never know. I've seen workmen leave their tools and things in our woodshed to save carrying them up and down the back lane. Somebody may have opened the door like that and let the goose out. I'm going to have a good look, anyhow!'

His brothers were manifestly impressed by Ron's new line of argument and straightway offered to join him in his quest. During the morning they searched in vain; but, the police having found no evidence of theft, they set out with new zest in the afternoon.

III

It was getting dusk when Mrs. Hume, looking anxiously from the front windows for some sign of her boys, beheld an extraordinary spectacle. The gate was suddenly flung wide open, and the boys, struggling frantically with the goose, entered in boisterous triumph. Ron was tugging at a cord attached to the unhappy bird's foot; Jack, walking beside it, was urging it forward by sundry prods and pushes; while little Keith was shooing it on from behind. All three were wildly excited.

'He was down among that clump of gum trees in the empty paddock at the corner of Montagu Street,' exclaimed Ron. 'My!' he continued, 'we've had a tussle to get him here!'

'Oh, well,' laughed their mother, proud of their exploit, 'we must get Dad to kill him as soon as we've had dinner; and then everybody must lend a hand with the plucking. We shall have him all ready for Christmas yet!'

We were a very merry party that night. The boys told the story of their adventure again and again, and each recital, revealing new details, produced fresh outbursts of laughter. We all did something towards making up for the hours that had been lost; by bedtime the goose, entirely innocent of feathers, looked like a poulterer's model; and we all crept off to our rooms feeling that the joy of Christmas had been considerably enhanced by the culprit who so carelessly opened the woodshed door.

IV

Next morning, however, the matter assumed a somewhat different aspect. The boys were astir at daylight, investigating the trail that Santa Claus had left. They appeared at breakfast loaded with toys, and wearing tissue paper caps—a helmet, a miter and a crown. Then, just as we were rising from table, Mrs. Hume, glancing at the window, espied the burly form of Superintendent Lewis coming up the drive.

'Well, to be sure!' she exclaimed in astonishment. 'Surely he could have left you alone on Christmas Day! Why on earth must he trouble you with Court business this morning?'

'It will be some very little thing,' her husband replied, soothingly. 'I expect he just requires my signature to some document or other. I'll answer the door myself!' And off he went. In five minutes he returned, bringing the police officer with him.

'I say!' he exclaimed, with a look compounded half of amusement and half of vexation. 'Here's a pretty kettle of fish! The Superintendent will tell you all about it.'

'Well, ma'am,' the officer began, bowing deferentially to Mrs. Hume, 'it's like this. Young Mr. and Mrs. Nelson, the newly-married couple that live in the red-brick villa near the corner of Montagu Street, had a goose sent them for Christmas, and, thinking it would be perfectly safe, they turned it loose in the vacant paddock next door. It seems that, late last night, Mr. Nelson glanced over the fence to see that it was all right, and found that it had disappeared. He reported it to us first thing this morning; we made enquiries; and—to make a long story short—we soon collected evidence to prove that these three young gentlemen were seen walking off with the missing goose! So I thought I'd better step round and see His Worship about it. He'll know what's best to be done!'

Keith, the youngest of the three brothers, burst into piteous lamentations, haunted, very possibly, by the prospect of spending Christmas Day in the cells. He may even have conjured up the vision—based on their overnight imaginings—of the three youthful thieves being hanged in front of the Nelson windows as the bride and bridegroom sat at their goose-less board. His brothers also looked distressingly glum, foreseeing, as the least of the dire consequences that must swiftly ensue, the loss of their own magnificent goose. Meanwhile, Mr. and Mrs. Hume, having withdrawn into an alcove, were engrossed in a whispered but earnest consultation.

'Oh, you couldn't, Fred,' I heard my hostess protest.

'It's all ready for cooking; for aught I know, it may even be in the oven. How could you send it now? And, besides, we have visitors. What could we possibly offer them for Christmas dinner if you send away the goose? Can't you buy one somewhere for the Nelsons?'

'I'm afraid it's rather too late for that,' the Mayor replied, looking as if the entire organization of the municipality had suddenly broken down. 'I haven't a notion in which direction to go in search of one; and by the time I got it, and took it to the Nelson's place, it would be of no use for today's dinner. I'll jump into the car and run round and see them about it! Come on. Superintendent. I'll drop you at your place on the way!'

V

In less than an hour he was back, laughing immoderately. He had evidently solved the problem to his own complete satisfaction.

'They're the jolliest young couple I've met for years!' he exclaimed, enthusiastically. 'They think it the biggest joke that has come to them since they married: they're just splitting their sides over it! I told them that, if they wished it, we'd send it round at once, or even cooked and ready for table; but they wouldn't hear of it. *He* said that he was mightily relieved at not having had to kill the creature; he'd never done such a thing in his life.

And *she* declared that she scarcely slept a wink the night before last through worrying about the cooking of it. She's a real Briton; you'd love her. She told me that we were not to worry a scrap. She had a lovely ham, she said, and *that* would perfectly satisfy them. And, as long as they lived, she assured me, every Christmas dinner would be made the merrier by the memory of their first. So what do you think I did—I hope you won't mind!'

'Asked them to dinner here, I suppose!' his wife hazarded, knowing him pretty well.

'Got it right first guess,' he laughed. 'Yes, they're coming! I'm to go back for them in an hour's time!'

That was one of the merriest Christmases that we spent in New Zealand. The bride and bridegroom entered into the spirit of the thing, and, displaying remarkable versatility, romped with the boys until bedtime. And, after the youngsters had said goodnight, they proved themselves, at the fireside, the most engaging and congenial companions.

Friendships were forged that Christmas Day that the years have strengthened and sweetened. The following Christmas Day was spent by the Nelsons very differently. There was no question of killing or cooking a goose, for Mrs. Nelson was in bed, proudly pressing to her breast the loveliest Christmas gift that could possibly have come to her. Early in the New Year Mr. and Mrs. Nelson joined the Church. 'It was absolutely the only thing that we could do,' the young mother told the old minister when he called to see them about it; 'the Humes have made religion seem so beautiful and so wonderful that we simply could not be left out in the cold—especially now that little Nora has come to us!'

VI

Twenty years later that same little Nora became the bride of Keith, the youngest of the Hume boys. To this day, the Christmas dinner is the event of the year with them all. From far and near they gather for that Yuletide feast. There is always a goose; and the goose is most carefully chosen and most vigilantly guarded. For the benefit of the younger members of the group, who have no personal recollection of the historic happening, the story of the celebrated adventure is annually recited, amidst appropriate ripples of Christmas merriment. Nobody listens more intently than Nora. Keith has a stock jibe that he whips out whenever he finds himself in the humor to tease his pretty young wife. 'I went out in search of *one* goose,' he will say, 'and lo and behold, I caught another!' But he wipes out the insult later on by proposing the health of *The Man Who Stole the Goose from the Woodshed*—a toast that, greeted by the entire company with tremendous enthusiasm, is always drunk with musical honors.

BROWN PAPER AND STRING

HOW MANY ACRES OF BROWN paper one wonders, and how many miles of string, are consumed in wrapping up the Christmas parcels? If all these crumpled sheets could afterwards be gathered up and pieced together, they would present a landscape that might be mistaken for the Sahara; while the string would several times girdle the globe. For, obviously, Christmastime is parcel-time. In this fundamental fact the essential genius, the inmost soul, of the festive season reveals itself. If a citizen of Mars visited this planet in December, nothing in our behavior would arrest his attention more forcibly than this sudden epidemic of parcels. Until a week or two before Christmas people consider it highly unbecoming to carry burdens of any kind. Then all at once the parcels appear! Day by day more and more people carry more and more parcels, until on Christmas Eve everybody is loaded with them! As Mr. C. J. Dennis sings:

> *All over the place they are today:*
> *Parcels sober and parcels gay,*
> *Smuggled in offices, borne up lifts—*

Oh, this is the day for Christmas gifts!
Parcels in tissue and parcels of brown.
Hurriedly rushed from the shops in town,
Secretly, furtively hidden away—
'Not to be opened till Christmas Day,'
Out 'mid the staid suburban homes
The delivery van insanely roams.
Motor cars and messenger boys
Bearing their burdens of Christmas joys—
Parcels, parcels, bulky and small
From a rocking horse to a rubber ball;
Parcels and paper and miles of string
In the service of Santa Claus, the King.

At Christmastime the jacaranda waves its graceful tassels of blue, the hydrangea is at the height of its glory, and brown paper and string become all the rage!

I

Even if a man had no calendar—and no children—to remind him that Christmas was coming, he would have no difficulty in detecting its footfall and discerning its approach. The shame of burdenbearing suddenly deserts men. The essential difference between the white man and the black man collapses. The black man is a born burden-bearer. He carries his load as naturally as a camel carries its hump; it seems to be part of him. But a white man bears a burden awkwardly, resentfully, shamefacedly. He regards it as a badge of servitude. He makes you feel that he was not made for it, nor it for him. Thus it comes about that, during fifty-one weeks of the year; a parcel is seldom a source of pride. If a lady enters a tramcar carrying a parcel, she does so apologetically, and seizes the first opportunity of explaining to a casual friend—in a voice that every other passenger can hear—the peculiar circumstances that have necessitated the humiliation.

But Christmastime changes everything. It is a carnival of brown paper and string. The streets are thronged with people carrying parcels of all sorts, shapes and sizes. In the tramcar the conspicuous passenger is not the passenger with the parcel, but the passenger with no parcel at all. At every stopping-place, the conductor helps a parcel-bedecked lady off the tram, and assists another, laden like a merchantman's camel, to board the car. And, although he shouts sternly, 'Hurry off, please!' and 'Hurry on, please!' you can, if you look closely, detect a smile tucked away under his moustache. For he himself has boys and girls at home; and it may be that, at this very moment, his own wife, with a big parcel under each arm, and a festoon of smaller ones hanging about her wrists and elbows, is being helped off some other tram by a comrade of the road.

II

Therein lies the social value of brown paper and string. They generate sympathy, goodwill and mutual understanding. If, when the conductor was helping one lady off the tram and another lady on, somebody had told him their names, the introduction would have been worthless. Names are strictly noncommittal; they are colorless; they do not help us to an intelligent knowledge of each other. But the parcels that the conductor hands to the ladies as they board and leave his car are much more lavish in their distribution of essential information. If the knowledge of the ladies' names is of any value to him, the conductor can obtain it instantaneously by simply glancing at the labels. He will probably do nothing of the kind, however; the parcels themselves will tell him things much more engrossing.

The foot of a wax doll protruding from one parcel conveys to his mind the picture of a laughing, girlish countenance that, bending over the face of a doll, takes to itself the pretty seriousness of fond, motherly solicitude. The handle of a cricket bat that has poked its way through the paper of another parcel summons to his fancy the roguish schoolboy features of a Test Match champion in the making; while a parcel from the poulterer's makes him feel as if he had peeped into the home just as the family was sitting down to the great dinner of the year. How such an introduction puts to shame the mere repetition of empty names! As the conductor hands the parcels to and fro, they chatter to him at the rate of nineteen to the dozen, and tell him all about the homes that they are so soon to gladden.

One of the most charming characteristics of these piles of parcels is that they open the way for the delicacies, the courtesies and the chivalries of life. One of the finest instances of this phenomenon occurs in the *Life of Sir Bartle Frere*, the celebrated ambassador. When Sir Bartle was returning to England after one of his diplomatic tours, it was the intention of Lady Frere to meet her husband at the train. At the last moment, however, she was prevented from doing so; and she had to send her coachman to the station alone. 'But, my lady,' the man protested, 'you forget that I have been engaged since Sir Bartle went abroad. How am I to recognize him?' 'Oh,' replied Lady Frere, 'that will be easy enough. Look out for a tall gentleman helping somebody!' And, surely enough, the coachman found Sir Bartle assisting an old lady from the carriage with her parcels!

III

Let no man suppose that, in writing of parcels, I am thinking merely of the contents of those parcels.

I am thinking not so much of the contents as of the brown paper and string. For it is the brown paper and string that make the parcel a parcel. Take away the brown paper and string, and the parcel is a parcel no longer. The doll wrapped up in brown paper and string is a parcel; the doll after the removal of the brown paper and string is simply a doll. That is why we always present the doll to the little girl with the brown paper and string still on it. In that way we provide her with two distinct and separate thrills—the thrill that arises from the parcel element and the thrill that arises from the doll element.

Every man, however matter-of-fact and prosaic, likes to receive his presents wrapped up in brown paper and string. He hesitates to cut the string; he prefers to untie the knot, to unfold the paper, and so to come slowly upon the fond surprise awaiting him. The contents element he will be able to enjoy for months, perhaps for years; the parcel element he can only enjoy for a few blissful seconds; he therefore lingers over it that he may taste its drawn out sweetness to the full. It is part—and a striking part—of our human love of mystery.

Like so many other things that are pregnant with romance, brown paper and string look commonplace enough; yet, in reality, they embody all the wistfulness, the tenderness and the sacredness of Christmastide. The emotions that, in the hearts alike of givers and receivers, will attend the opening of the parcels, represent the condensed essence of that peace and goodwill of which the angels caroled, while the rustling of all these acres of brown paper, properly heard and accurately interpreted, is itself an essential fragment of the heavenly melodies.

There is one respect in which that first and greatest of all Christmas gifts resembles these parcels of ours. What is it that we sing at Christmastime?

> *Veiled in flesh the Godhead see,*
> *Hail the Incarnate Deity!*

I have an old hymnbook in which the words are rendered:

> *Wrapped in flesh the Godhead see,*
> *Hail the Incarnate Deity!*

Wrapped in flesh! It is the phraseology of the parcel! The child's eyes sparkle as he catches a glimpse of the present through the paper. Human eyes have been entranced as they have beheld the unspeakable gift '*wrapped in flesh*'—the Deity Incarnate! They have never gazed upon its unveiled splendor. But they cherish in their hearts a wondrous secret. They know that the great manifestation is coming. They shall see Him as He is; they shall gaze with open face upon the glory ineffable; and even Christmastime can bring to men no expectation more radiant than that.

THE INVISIBLE CHILDREN

AT THIS TIME OF THE YEAR there are children everywhere. They crowd the pavements; they throng the shops; they seem to feel that, at Christmastime, the world belongs to them.

I

Mingling with this surging concourse of youngsters are the invisible children; and the invisible children are the most lovable children of all, laughing-eyed and tousle-headed boys; girls with flaxen hair and dimpled cheeks; each is the perfect pattern of all that a child should be.

They cost nothing. They eat no food, wear out no clothes and break no toys. They are never troublesome and never ill. They are enrolled at no school; no Registrar of Births, Marriages and Deaths has any record of their names. As a matter of fact, they have no names, for, with the characteristic forgetfulness of childhood, they have forgotten to be born.

They are quite invisible. At least, each is visible to only one pair of eyes. But to that one pair of doting eyes each represents the quintessence of perfection. To those eyes there never was, and never can be, a child of such winsomeness and charm and grace as the child who, invisible to everybody but themselves, is the idol of their ceaseless devotion.

II

For the invisible children are the children of all lonely men and lonely women, the children of their dreams and of their fancies, the children that will never be born. They are the sons and daughters of the solitary, the children that, in rapturous moments of wonder and wistfulness, they glimpse through the mist of the years.

These children are invisible to ordinary eyes; but just once or twice the lips of their fond parents have become unsealed, and we have almost caught sight of them. Let us take a couple of examples. The one shall be the case of a man; the other the case of a woman.

In his *Life of Francis Assisi,* Professor J. Herkless tells how, at one stage, Francis was torn between the monastic life on the one hand and the domestic life on the other. He longed to be a friar and to dedicate himself to poverty and pilgrimage; and yet he loved a sweet and noble and gracious woman. He wrestled with his alternatives, and, at length, through an agony of tears, he chose the cloak and the cowl.

But still the lovely face haunted him by cloister and by shrine. And one radiant moonlit night, when the earth was wrapped in snow, the brethren of the monastery saw him rise at dead of night. He crept out into the grounds and, in the soft, silvery moonlight, fashioned out of the snow with deft, artistic fingers the images of a lovely woman and four beautiful children.

He arranged them in a circle, sat with them for a while, and, giving rein to his fancy, tasted for one delicious hour the joys of hearth and home. Then, solemnly rising, he bade them all an agonizing and final farewell, renounced such ecstasies forever and reentered the monastery. That night the deep, impressive eyes of one of earth's purest and noblest saints looked full into the fair face of the Child Invisible.

III

For womanhood, let Ada Cambridge speak. In *The Hand in the Dark and Other Verses* she has a touching little poem that she calls *The Virgin Martyr*. It might just as well have been called 'The Invisible Child.'

> *Every wild she-bird has nest and mate in the*
> *warm April weather,*
> *But a captive woman, made for love,*
> *no mate, no nest, has she.*

In the spring of young desire,
young men and maids are wed together,
And the happy mothers flaunt their bliss f
or all the world to see.
Nature's sacramental feast for them
—an empty board for me.

I, a young maid once, an old maid now,
deposed, despised, forgotten,
I, like them, have thrilled with passion
and have dreamed of nuptial rest,
Of the trembling life within me
of my children unbegotten,
Of a breathing new-born body
to my yearning bosom prest,
Of the rapture of a little soft mouth
drinking at my breast.

Time, that heals so many sorrows,
keeps mine ever-freshly aching.
Though my face is growing furrowed
and my brown hair turning white.
Still I mourn my irremediable loss, asleep or waking;
Still I hear my son's voice calling '
Mother' in the dead of night,
And am haunted by my girl's eyes
that will never see the light.

O my children that I might have had!
My children lost forever!

O the goodly years that might have been,
now desolate and bare!
O God, what have I lacked, what have I done,
that I should never
Take my birthright like the others,
take the crown that women wear,

And possess the common heritage
to which all flesh is heir?

IV

But, whether a man or a woman is concerned, the point is that the Invisible Child is a very beautiful child. He is absolutely without faults or flaws or disfigurements of any kind. He is, to the last decimal point, all that his father, his mother, would have him to be.

And he has a great work to do in the world. He will either sweeten the life of that desolate father or mother of his or else make it as bitter as wormwood. He will wonderfully soften or cruelly harden them.

For the Invisible Child calls his solitary father or lonely mother to the service of the world's childhood. He needs no food nor clothing; so they, for his sake, can feed and clothe the child who has no parents to feed and clothe him.

He needs no fatherly wisdom nor motherly tenderness; so they can keep their wisdom wise and their tenderness tender by fathering and mothering the child whose pitiful plight leaves him in desperate need of just such help. The Invisible Child needs no sweets, no tops, no dolls, no balls; so they can see that the birthdays of the visible child are made glad, and, at Christmastime, his stocking filled.

Josephine Butler had an invisible child. Only, in her case, the invisible child had once been visible. We all remember, with a shudder, the story of that holiday—the father and mother in Europe, the little girlie left at home. And at last the night came when father and mother were expected. And in the night there was the sound of wheels and the commotion in the great hall below. The excited little daughter sprang from her bed, rushed out into the corridor, jumped up on to the banister rail to peer over and see 'Dadda' and 'Mamma' again. And then—the lost balance! The awful fall! 'Never,' says Mrs. Butler, 'never can I lose that memory, the fall, the sudden cry, and then the silence. It was pitiful to see her, helpless in her father's arms, her little drooping head resting on his shoulder, and her beautiful golden hair, all stained with blood, falling over his arm. Would to God that I had died that death for her! If only we had been permitted one look, one moment of recognition!' Here, then, is a picture from life of the Invisible Child. And we all know what resulted. Mrs. Josephine Butler could find no comfort until she rose from her grief and devoted herself to all the wayward and motherless daughters of the great world outside, and everybody who knows the story of that greatly heroic life for the world's wayward womanhood thanks God for that Invisible Child. Such invisible children call, not for sorrow, but for service.

It is a great thing for the world that there are men and women with no children of their own. For there are children without fathers and without mothers, and there are children who would be better off if they had none.

The lonely men and women are called by the Invisible Child to devote their lives to the service of the lonely children. And, in ministering to the world's childhood, they will lose their loneliness and their longing, for the Invisible Child will become incarnate in the children around them; and listening to his song and his laughter, they will drink the rich red wine of a full-orbed life after all.

THE LOST CHRONICLES OF SUFI-ABBAS

WHO WOULD SUSPECT THAT THIS tall and handsome figure, robed in the glowing and colorful draperies of the East, and talking fluently in their own tongues to the Orientals that swarm about him, is, in reality, no Asiatic at all?

I

In the bustling courtyard of a big box-like hostelry in Ispahan, this electric personality moves among merchants, officials and slaves with the air of a man who is accustomed to having his every command instantly obeyed.

His voice, though savoring slightly of shrillness, is vibrant with self-confidence and sharp with authority. His orders ring out like pistol shots.

History knows this man as Marco Polo, the renowned traveler of Venice. Glance at him again. He is in earnest, and even excited, conversation with the innkeeper.

'If,' he exclaims decisively, 'if I have to search through every town from Bagdad to Samarkand, and even if it costs me my last camel and my last roll of silk, I will find the lost chronicles of Sufi-Abbas, the astrologer, and bring to light the missing links in the story!'

The story that he had in mind was, of course, the story of the Three Wise Men. By studying carefully such records as had come to hand, and by talking with Eastern scholars in their palm-shaded gardens and bustling bazaars, Marco Polo had unearthed many of the graphic details of the intriguing tale, but some essential fragments still eluded him.

II

In March 1272—the month of the devastating earthquake at Yarad-haifa—an old priest at Persepolis, a wizened little creature with a long, grizzly beard, who wore fantastic yellow robes and was almost blind as a result of some horrible disease the ravages of which disfigured his entire countenance, told him that much of the information that he sought was to be found in the chronicles of Sufi-Abbas, the astrologer of Carmana.

'Then, cost the journey what it may, I will find them!' cried Marco Polo eagerly; and, surely enough, less than a year later, among the flotsam and jetsam offered for sale by a disreputable old dealer at Singara, not far from the banks of the Tigris, he unearthed the faded and tattered roll of parchments for which he had so diligently sought.

It is characteristic of Marco Polo that, having secured the grimy document on which he had set such extraordinary value, he took little or no further interest in it. He never coordinated the literary morsels that he had with such pains collected; and, since the scrolls that he gathered were soon afterwards scattered or destroyed, the world is very little the wiser as a result of his researches. But, in his later days, he often discussed the matter with his daughters, Fantina, Bellela and Moreta; these, in turn, repeated the story to their children; and little by little, the graceful tradition that they unfolded took to itself a definite shape.

III

Marco Polo discovered, so these Oriental ladies averred, that the Three Wise Men were three kings, differing the one from the other as sharply and as strikingly as any three individuals could possibly do. In scarcely one respect did any member of the imposing trio resemble either of his companions.

Gaspar, King of hoary Tarshish, was young and tall, straight as an arrow and black as ebony.

Balthazar, King of ancient Chaldea, was middle-aged and bearded, of medium height and olive-skinned.

Melchior, King of Nubia, was very old and very pale, of short stature, withered, infirm and bent.

If the story, as Fantina, the eldest daughter of Marco Polo passed it on to her offspring, is to believed, the travelers had not gone far before ill-fortune overtook them. Gaspar's camel trod upon a viper in the thick undergrowth on the fringe of the desert. The reptile fastened upon the tender part of the animal's foot; in an hour or two the limb was too swollen and inflamed to permit further progress; and, in the grey of the following dawn, the camel died.

What was to be done? Balthazar and Melchior were as grieved and as troubled as was Gaspar himself. But they pointed out that the Star would not stand still in the sky because a snake had killed a camel among the sands. Somebody must follow the celestial guide. Better that two should find the new king than that all three should be whelmed in failure and disappointment. Gaspar sorrowfully agreed. 'Anyway,' he added, his black face brightening with a brave smile, 'I am young and strong; I am accustomed to walking long distances. I will follow the trail of your camels, and, it may be that, in spite of my loss, I, too, may find the King!'

Balthazar and Melchior thereupon bade him a sad farewell and set off by themselves, leaving Gaspar to follow as best he could on foot. But, when that day's sun set in splendor over the western horizon, they looked for the star but for some time failed to discern it. It had become so faint that they had to strain their eyes to detect it. And the next night it vanished altogether.

Mortified and disgusted, they abandoned the quest and started on their return journey. In due course they met Gaspar struggling cheerfully on. He was surprised to see them, and still more astonished when they told their tale.

'Lost the star!' he cried incredulously. 'Why, nonsense! There it is!' And there, surely enough, it was!

They then resolved to journey together, sharing the benefit of the two surviving camels. Sometimes two of them mounted the stronger camel; sometimes Gaspar rode and Balthazar walked beside him; sometimes Balthazar rode the camel while Gaspar resumed his weary trudge; and now and again even Melchior, aged and infirm as he was, insisted on hobbling along on foot, while the two younger men rested. But, however they disposed themselves, the star shone brightly on until, in due course, it brought them to the inn in which the young child lay.

And so these pilgrim kings learned that they who follow the star become, in virtue of that circumstance, members one of another. The sorrows of one become the sorrows of all: the privileges of one become the privileges of all. Those who think only of themselves, and who display no sympathy with a less fortunate companion, soon lose the heavenly vision. But when each bravely shares the afflictions of those who have been overtaken by disaster, the star blazes like an oriflamme in the eastern sky.

IV

It was quite a different experience that intrigued Bellela, Marco Polo's second daughter, and that she most stressed to her children. It seems that, while resting amidst the shades of a green and hospitable oasis, the three pilgrims began to speculate, as was natural, concerning the appearance of Him to whom their celestial guide was leading them. They agreed that He would be stately and regal and grand, noble in bearing and wise in speech. But of what color?

Gaspar felt certain that he would be black. 'Long before any of your paler civilizations began,' he claimed, 'there dwelt, far back among the forests of the south, black nations of infinite power and inscrutable wisdom. One of these days when the world is wide open, and when the secrets of its remote past are clearly read, humanity will discover with astonishment that vast empires were erected by men of dusky skin while the rest of the world was buried in slumber and stagnation. I believe,' he concluded, 'that He to whom the star is leading us has come to restore to our peoples their ancient glory!'

Balthazar brushed aside the preposterous theory with impatience. He was sure that the Divine One to whom they were being led would have a skin of olive-colored hue. 'Everybody knows,' he insisted, 'that all the world's most famous dreamers and sages and poets have dwelt in the East. And if, of late, the prophetic fires have died down, it is only that they may blaze up again with richer splendor than ever in this Heavenly Prophet to whom we are being guided.'

'All that you say is true,' exclaimed old Melchior in quiet and unimpassioned tones, 'and yet I feel that you must both be disappointed. Perhaps because my eyes are so soon to close for ever, I seem to scan the years that are coming more clearly than you do. And, looking down the avenue of the centuries-to-be, I see that the white races are to rise to a grandeur and an authority that they have never yet known. And somehow, I feel that this thing that is just about to happen is the crisis of human destiny, the turning point of the ages! I believe that we are being led to the Creator of a New Era—and a white one!'

From quiet reasoning and abstract speculation they soon passed to argument and angry contention. Each claimed for his own section of mankind virtues and achievements to which the others could never pretend; and each poured upon the others the vials of bitter contempt and withering derision. But while they argued, the shadows lengthened and the dusk fell.

'I have no patience with either of you!' cried Gaspar, fiercely springing to his feet. 'I am sick of your absurdities! I am going to resume the journey. You can come or stay as you will; it is nothing to me!' The others flung their taunts after him; but they, too, moved towards the camels.

When they were ready to start, however, they each made separately a discovery that filled all three with consternation and dismay. Where was the star? There was no sign of it! And, without it, how could they proceed?

The catastrophe that had overtaken them filled their hearts with fellow feeling and with sympathy for one another. In this new situation, they forgot the cruel words that each had spoken and, secretly ashamed of all that had been said in the course of their wordy warfare, each went out of his way to show kindness and consideration to the others. And as, in their hearts, a new and fonder comradeship was born, the star gradually reappeared in the heavens. They saluted it with gladness, and followed it in peace and mutual goodwill until, in due course, it brought them to the little inn at Bethlehem.

V

But Moreta, the youngest of Marco Polo's daughters, fastened upon a very different aspect of the great adventure and made the most of it in telling the tale to her children. For, just as the three kings differed in age, in color, and in outward appearance, so they differed also in relation to their secret thoughts, emotions and aspirations.

Gaspar, the youthful King of Tarshish, set out on his quest hoping that the star would lead him to a *king*. The world, he felt, wanted a master, a sovereign, a ruler, a lord. And, longing for such a lord, Gaspar took with him a tribute of gold, a royal gift.

Balthazar, the mature King of Chaldea, hoped that the star would lead him to a *God*. He had lived long enough to realize that behind the seen lies the unseen. And yet, like most men in middle-life, he had come to feel that he had lost the vision of those intangible realities. Youth is spiritually minded and age is spiritually minded; but middle-age is tyrannized by the senses. Material things dominate the soul. Youth will fling everything to the winds to follow an ideal, and will count the world well lost for the joy of realizing the fulfilment of a dream. Age recognizes that the veil between the worlds is wearing thin, and will treat every thought of eternal things with reverence. But middle-age is monopolized by money and pride and worldly ambition. Yet middle-age sometimes becomes conscious, at least for a moment, of the dangerous condition into which it has drifted.

Balthazar had some such consciousness. Whenever he sought to probe the mysteries of the invisible, his mind became confused. What is God? Where is God? *'Oh, that I knew where I might find Him!'* And thirsting for God as the deer thirsts for the waterbrooks, longing for God as blind men long for light, Balthazar answered the challenge of the star. And he took with him a tribute of incense—frankincense—with which to worship.

And Melchior, the aged King of Nubia longed for a *Savior*. After the fashion of old men, his mind dwelt in the years that were past. And he felt—felt increasingly—that those years were sadly stained, their record tragically smudged. And soon, he realized, he must pass into the great unknown with much of guilt upon his conscience. Was there no priest by whom his iniquity could be absolved, no sacrifice by which his transgression could be removed, no fountain in which his soul could be eternally cleansed? And, hoping fervently that the star might lead him to a Savior—a Savior who, he instinctively felt, must of necessity be a sufferer—he took with him his gift of myrrh.

VI

And so they came to Bethlehem. And when they saw that the star had but led them to a baby in a woman's arms, all three were at first overwhelmed with chagrin and dismay. But, as they sat and pondered this strange happening, they heard Mary, after the fashion of mothers, singing to her child. And all three listened.

'My soul doth magnify the Lord!' she sang. 'The Lord!' exclaimed Gaspar. 'Then I have found my Sovereign, my Monarch, my King, my Lord!' And he offered his gold. But Mary sang on.

'And my spirit hath rejoiced in God...' she continued. *'In God!'* cried Balthazar, his face lighting up. 'Then I have found Him—the God for whom my spirit hungered!' And he presented his incense to the babe. But not even yet had Mary finished her song.

'My soul doth magnify the Lord and my spirit hath rejoiced in God my Savior!' *'My Savior!'* echoed Melchior, *'My Savior!'* And he offered his vase of myrrh.

And so Gaspar found in Jesus the King of his desire. And Balthazar found in Jesus the God he had so passionately sought. And Melchior found in Jesus the Savior for whom his very soul was aching.

Every man finds in Jesus exactly what he most needs. That is the essence of the Christmas story; and that is the essence of the everlasting gospel.

ABOUT THE COVER

DESTINY HANGS ON A FLOWER in *A Midsummer's Christmas.* As an unashamed romantic, how could I not like a story about a lonely man's use of a nasturtium to get someone's attention? For the pivotal role it plays in this delightful tale, its colorful blooms earn a place on the back cover.

Laura Zugzda, the cover designer, rightly observed that of all possible images one of a book is an obvious choice given the title. The bright light and stars convey a little of the gracious and wonderful meditations on the season.

The cool colors on the front contrast with the warm ones on the back. As pointed out in "A Midsummer's Christmas," it's natural for some of us to think of the "bleak midwinter," but for others Christmas comes in summer.

—Michael Dalton

PUBLISHER'S NOTE

WE ARE GRATEFUL to Dr. Frank Rees at Whitley College for the permission to publish this book and for the practical support given by the College.

A portion of the sale of each book will go toward the training of pastors and missionaries at Whitley College, a ministry that F. W. Boreham supported during his lifetime.

Sincere thanks to Laura Zugzda for cover design and Marcia Breece for layout.

Further information about the life and work of F. W. Boreham is available at the F. W. Boreham Facebook page: http://www.facebook.com/pages/F-W-Boreham/121475236386.

Please address any comments and questions to:

Geoff Pound
24 Montana Street
GLEN IRIS
Australia 3146
+61 (0) 417 485200
geoffpound@gmail.com

Jeff Cranston
LowCountry Community Church
801 Buckwalter Parkway
Bluffton, SC 29910
jcranston@lowcountrycc.org
www.lowcountrycc.org

Michael Dalton
2163 Fern Street
Eureka, CA 95503
(707) 442-8967
dalton.michael@sbcglobal.net

We enjoy hearing from people. Tell us a story.

Printed in Great Britain
by Amazon

46120145R00067